PRAISE FOR POETRY BY JANE MARLA ROBBINS

The Topanga Poems: Fifteen Years in the Canyon
"Vibrant.... A remarkable poem log."
W.S. Merwin, U.S. Poet Laureate, 1952, 2010

Poems of The Laughing Buddha
"Lively, cerebral, witty, yet filled with profound reflections, Robbins' work reminds us that poetry can be both a celebration and an entertainment – not to mention food for thought."
Patricia Bosworth, *Vanity Fair* contributing Editor, author of *Anything Your Little Heart Desires* and *The Men in My Life*

"In these brightly lit and joy-filled poems, all inspired by a stone stature of the Laughing Buddha, the poet practically dares the universe to bring her down, and it cannot do so. In poem after poem, laughter triumphs over whatever comes her way, and it is a literate, knowing laughter, a cosmic, Buddhist laughter that will make even the most jaded reader say with the poet, 'Okay, I'm smiling now./ Okay, I'll have fun. With you. FUN!' "
Gail Wronsky, poet, author of *Blue Shadow Behind Everything Dazzling* and *Dying For Beauty*

"Lucky Buddha to find a home in Jane Marla Robbins' Topanga Canyon garden, and have her take down his every wise word. Her poems will set you smiling, then laughing, then seeing, then smiling a deeper kind of smile. Step into her garden and make your day."
John Guare, playwright, Pulitzer Prize, Finalist, *House of Blue Leaves* and *Six Degrees of Separation.*

Café Mimosa in Topanga

"*Café Mimosa in Topanga* is a lively, elegiac dance, full of love and healing."

Aram Saroyan, author of *Complete Minimal Poems*, William Carlos Williams Award and *Day and Night: Bolinas Poems*

"Jane Marla Robbins, poet and Topanga shaman, journeys her readers, as the café does its regulars, out of their hunger and loneliness and into fullness and happiness. The poems are elegantly crafted, smart and deep."

Peter Angelo Simon, photographer, author of *Big Apple Circus* and *Muhammad Ali Fighter's Heaven 1974*

"These are poems of Place, composed with deceptively perceptive observations, which makes them a pleasure to read."

Michael C. Ford, author of *Language Commando*, Grammy nomination

"The writing is nourishment. And moving. I want to go to the café – although I feel that I have already been there."

Pamela Shaw, actor, *Lucky Stiff* and *The Whistleblower*

"Throughout *Café Mimosa in Topanga* Jane Marla Robbins reminds us we're all lucky enough to have places in our lives that rise from the prosaic to the poetic. It's a place we all need."

David Finkle, author of *People Tell Me Things* and *The Man With the Overcoat*

CAFÉ MIMOSA IN TOPANGA

ALSO BY JANE MARLA ROBBINS

Poems of The Laughing Buddha

Dogs in Topanga

Acting Techniques for Everyday Life:
Look and Feel Self-Confident in
Difficult Real Life Situations

Perform at Your Best:
Acting Techniques for Business,
Social and Personal Success

CAFÉ MIMOSA
IN TOPANGA

Poems by

JANE MARLA ROBBINS

SHINING TREE PRESS

CAFÉ MIMOSA IN TOPANGA

ISBN 978-0-692-87042-6

Published in the United States

Library of Congress Control Number:
2017900939

Shining Tree Press
20621 Callon Drive
Topanga, California 90290

The names of people, places and things have not been changed,
in order to celebrate and protect the innocent.

DEDICATION

This book is dedicated to Arlette Parker, who was the first to have a vision for the café, built it up from scratch in 1992, and somehow left in it her own feisty French charm and good humor; and to Claire Denis who, eleven years later, bought it, put her own French stamp on it, and who, in the thirteen years since then, has made it a haven for so many, bringing disparate people together in a sweet and healing place, where they not only get along, but are also glad to be there. Together.

CONTENTS

Foreword   11

Café Mimosa   13
Mimosa Morning   15
French   18
Mother's Day Morning   20
Edible Landscapes   26
Animal Talk   29
A Shirt   30
Limerickish   31
Letting Go The Metronome   32
Juggling   34
Dave Lichten, 1946–2015   36
Dream Catchers   37
How Many Languages   38
A Wedding   39
Closing Time   42
Presidential Election   44

My Thanks   51
About the Author   53
A Recording   55

FOREWORD

I live in Topanga Canyon. California. I have lived here since 1992. Twenty-four years. Almost a quarter of a century.

The people who live here include homeless creekers, multi-millionaires, and everything in-between. We live here because we love the often wild and always gorgeous nature that surrounds us: majestic green mountains; waterfalls; fields full of wild flowers in spring and a few wild animals (coyotes, deer, an occasional mountain lion—although my neighbor had one for a pet a while ago).

The people who live here love it here. We'd have to love it. Topanga is also famous for its wildfires. We're perhaps an odd bunch. But we're a merry one.

In the middle of the canyon sits the Café Mimosa that these poems, written between 2015 and 2016, describe. I understand that this book may be as much a portrait of me as it is of the café. Still, I hope some of the essence of Mimosa and its cast of characters comes through, delights, edifies, and even awakens some special part of you – as it has for me.

JMR

CAFÉ MIMOSA

January 18, 2015

Rainy afternoon.
Only the desperate regulars.
Josiah, who drives a bus for a living,
John, who drives a car for a living,
and Tony, driven by seemingly
super-human energy
to find more water-dropping helicopters
to keep us safe from fires.
Of course it's raining today
so it's moot.

None of these three men speaks
in cadences I'm used to:
John, with puns and jokes
and Tony almost faster than a person can follow.
"I'm not going to talk about myself anymore,"
he tells me five times,
"I'm not going to talk about myself anymore,"
talking of course about himself,
his smart, driven self.

Josiah's index finger follows and follows
and follows the wicker border
of the table where he's sitting,
his focus, laser-like, and I wonder:

Is it his crystal ball?
I finally ask him what he's looking at.
"A baby cockroach trapped under the wicker,"
he says, explaining how food inevitably
gets caught and buried there.

We are all trapped, sometimes, I think, looking for food,
and for all of us there is someone watching,
maybe to free us,
maybe to help, maybe to laugh.
We are not alone.

MIMOSA MORNING

We're lonely. We're all so lonely.
I came here naked in my loneliness,
right out of bed,
my dog not company enough.

People recognize me here,
some say they read and love my books,
I am a sponge for being seen,
desperate to be part of the human race and world.

Two men I've known casually for years
but whose names I do not know
look gentle this morning, gentle, inviting.
The first, whom I encounter in the parking lot,
with a new white beard that makes him look
like a guru or shaman, is all at once so open, loving
and accessible that I feel myself crying when we hug,
not sobbing, but feeling calming gentle waves
of relief through my body, not a tsunami, just a few tears,
water on my cheeks. Perhaps we are both surprised.
Perhaps we are both lonely.

Once inside, pouring my coffee, we hug again,
and then the second man, taller, sunburnt,
attractive in a way that says his body makes things,
athletic and strong, whose name, even after seeing him
for fifteen years in the canyon, I do not know,
comes in for another hug. The third hug.
And I am moved by the spongy softness

of our bodies coming together,
again feel the tears coming.

Where does this happen? Maybe only
at a café named Mimosa
(After a sweet smelling flower?
Or is it an alcoholic concoction?).
And then I see the man I'm hugging, softly and strongly,
(although only with one arm,
Dancer's leash is in my other hand) –
this man has shed tears too.
Not a lot, maybe only two or three.
But I'm shocked, enlightened, fed, jubilant, amazed.
A morning of three musketeers! What a place.

Tommy Teeple (surely that's a made up name) comes by;
his business card boasts "Edible Landscapes;"
and though I seem to have forgotten his name
somehow I remember my garden
and the dead rose bush in front of my house
which needs its roots removed,
and I remember the two succulents I bought yesterday
and think that they could live in its place,
the grey of their grey-green leaves
a little like the color of my aluminum house.
And the next thing you know, he says he can come by
right now, with Claudio, to dig out the dead roots
and put in the two new plants.
He comes, and it turns out we both have potting soil.

So the extraction and the planting take place,
the mulching and the watering,
and these two new men are making my garden grow,
not with roses (not in this drought!)
but with succulents that need so much less water,
native to our desert of angels.

First, this morning, there was drought and famine,
the dryness of loneliness, a starving of the human spirit.
But a jump in the car and a trip to Mimosa
has watered barren land
so that flowers, again,
can grow.

FRENCH

Claire owns the café
and made the hats for sale on the far wall,
a purple cloche with a turquoise band,
a yellow sun hat with a purple bow.

Claire is French. *Elle parle français. Elle parle anglais.*
She speaks English. She speaks French
and I speak French with her. Sometimes.
(A perfect eighth grade French.
Though I understand only the tiniest amount of what she says!)

"Je l'aime ici! Je l'aime ici!"
"I love it here! I love it here!"
which people may think can mean the same thing,
but it's possible their meanings may be
wildly, subtly different, just as French music,
French history and French DNA are different
from our Anglo Saxon's.

Maybe words never really catch
what we mean, anyway. Clearer always, surely,
are smiling eyes in contact with ours, or a hug,
or a cup of coffee (with or without milk and sugar)
where the meaning although possibly fleeting
is, in its own way, probably better digested.
And if it's made with love – Ah!

So could it really be an accident
the Frenchies' word for coffee is café

which in English, as in French,
means both the caffeinated drink
AND the establishment where you can drink it?
Ah, the joke, sweet as a mocha shake,
this sleight of words, this *jeu de mots*,
little double entendre!

So that CAFÉ MIMOSA could be
a blossoming tree of a café,
or a café which includes a flowering tree,
or a type of coffee made from flowers.
Ah.

MOTHER'S DAY MORNING

Claire isn't here. She is the mother here and absent,
      like my own, gone now almost five years,
      and still I talk to her, maybe more than I did
      when she was alive. I miss the structure
      of her being here. Not the wilder storms.

The felt hats on the soft shelf by the wall,
      like good mothers, remind us to keep safe:
            to keep us warm if it's cold,
      or, if it's hot, to protect us from the sun.

When I walk in, the wild-haired regulars, all men,
      are at the big table: revolutionary radicals all,
            except for maybe the wooden flute player
      whom I've seen for years, playing everywhere,
in parking lots, outside the Topanga Thrift Store,
      wide-eyed like a child needing mothering.
            And who does not.

Where are the mothers? Mostly not here, not today;
      but the mother energy envelops us,
      with gentle pillows on hugging couches,
      lavender conditioning shampoos for sale
      and big linen napkins embroidered with
            lucky ladybugs.

There are even books to feed you
along with the muffins, the salads, the specials:
      gluten-free bread with avocado or salmon,
      and two organic, home made soups.

Debby, the dancer/writer, edits at the far table,
her flowered dress almost matching the chrysanthemum
lampshade,
and perhaps it's a perfect Mother Oak that's painted
in milky white on the front window.

On the counter are packs of Angel Cards
(What Mommy doesn't have all your answers?)
and other decks as well: The Couples Quiz and The Perfect Match,
all answering your most pressing questions,
answers any perfect mother'd know.

The books I wrote are there: *Dogs in Topanga;*
Acting Techniques for Everyday Life;
Poems of The Laughing Buddha –
the place embraces these, my children
(as a perfect mother would),
as well as books by other writers from Topanga:
David Kearney, Rachel Resnick and Hope Edelman.

Today there's avocado zucchini soup,
its veggies all from local gardens,
even as Mother Earth gives us our food,
gives us, too, something to stand on,
grow from, even as our mothers do and did,
our umbilical cord to Earth a powerful imperative.

The magazines here promise to nourish our minds, even our souls:
from Live Happily, to *Bon Appétit* to *Vanity Fair;*
and there are board games too

because as every mother knows: her children
need to play.

People come here for play, for friendship, for work,
sending emails, making plans, writing scripts
and books and poems,
this place gives birth to it all, inspires,
nourishes, feeds,
to the quiet metronomic tap dance of computers.

NOW, WHERE IS THAT TUMERIC SOUP?!

Behind the counter, young Alexandra, today's
mother surrogate,
doe-eyed, mini-skirted, hair in a bob, serves only
until noon,
waiting for her own mother to celebrate
their Mother's Day.

After I name my soup (Oops, I changed my mind --
I'll have the avocado zucchini)
Alex and I improvise a song about how I want it:
"Chilled or warm?" she warbles.
"Chilled or warm?" I soprano back,
and the duet continues, back and forth
and back and forth
as we laugh back and forth and back and forth,
then hug the warm and tight embrace that all of us
probably wanted from our mothers.

Here, I feel not everyone got such a hug.

And it's never too late. Not here. Here,
where you can get
tamales courtesy of "Adriana's Mom,"
Mother energy everywhere:
for Pete's sake, on the shelf with the soaps for sale is
"Mongolian Mare's Milk Soap," Mother's milk
is everywhere,
the pillows on the couches, mommy breasts.

A woman enters with her husband and her son,
a loving mother, we hope; they are quiet.
It is perhaps a sacred holiday for them.
Possibly for this café. Possibly for the earth.

On the far shelf there's a deck of Tarot cards,
as if you could divine the answers to
Did we choose our mothers before we came here
so we could learn our special hard-edged lessons?
or
Are our mothers simply appropriate rewards
or punishments for what we did in yet another life?

I bring my dog, I am allowed; I have a license.
Am I his mother? Certainly I take care of him:
feed him, wash him, as if he were my child.
His coat today is one half lamb-like curls,
one half frizz:
who was his mother? Does it matter? He's mine now,

takes care of me, washes me with kisses, feeds me
with kindnesses in ways my mother never could.

John, brilliant, always with a new career
(cooking, computers, driving, you name it)
feeds us with his humor, wit and verbal games,
notes my dog's "self-denigrating humor."
I raise an eyebrow; he raises the ante, says,
"Self-defecating humor?" and then I dare
to say out loud,
"Was that a projection?" then segue with
"WHAT IS NOT A PROJECTION?!"

Perhaps I don't really see Mimosa,
only project my own concerns onto the walls,
where sometimes there are paintings, but not today.
Maybe I project my own desires on the books and cards,
project my inner appetites onto the menu
(Could I be seeking baby food?),
onto the chai lattes, cappuccinos, café lattes,
all mother's milk, this Mother's Day,
and I am beyond grateful I have this womb to come to.

Soon a mother with her son sits by the front window, quiet.
He, a teenager, bored. She, with a tarot deck in her hands:
Will it tell her the mystery of her motherhood,
how it comes to pass that our universe insists on
multiplying itself, fornicating, giving birth?
His hair is thick, she's wearing hers in six-inch pigtails
(I notice the hairy resemblance).

She's dressed in black, one thigh crossed over the other leg,
he's slouched down, wearing greys:
nothing black or white when you're only thirteen.

A man takes his little daughter to the bathroom,
the Ladies Room key attached to a metal spoon.
Daddies can be mommies: my neighbor
stayed home with his new daughter
every day for two years while the mother was at work,
he, a good mommy: once, I saw him give the little girl a bath,
how he folded her in his arms, one hand softly holding
the top of her head, as if she were embraced
in a cocoon,
a Native American papoose: surely a memory to keep her sane
for the rest of her life.
Our mothering comes from everywhere.

And from everywhere here I am nourished and fed,
even by the colors of Mimosa's walls:
half of the café is painted yellow, like the sun,
the orb that keeps us all alive
(another umbilical mystery);
the other half is painted blue,
like the sky that holds the sun in its course,
or is it some gravitational cycling that keeps everything turning,
as I imagine the turning of a baby in its mother's womb,
a little every time the mother moves –
when she picks something up,
or when she lies down, or finally,
gives birth.

EDIBLE LANDSCAPES

Tommy Teeple, a regular, his brown curls
like the corkscrew tendrils of my favorite pea pods,
carries a business card that reads
"Edible Landscapes."
Just when you thought that gardens were designed
only to offer decoration and beauty to the world,
Tommy plants you one to eat;
so just as beauty might nourish your soul,
his gardens feed your stomach;
and looking at one of his landscapes could be
like looking into your very own cupboard
(Things are rarely what they seem).

You start with dirt and seeds,
then witness shoots, flowers, fruits – –
our own life's journey
right in your own backyard.

Mimosa, too, is an edible landscape –
and though you could eat
the lavender and rosemary outside by the porch,
inside: could you also eat
the red and gold armchair?
Ah, yes - with your eyes!

Take Susan, today's barista, she's got
thick, magenta dreadlocks made of knobby yarn
almost three feet long, which,

depending on your point of view,
could indeed seem "good enough to eat;"
while the dramatic tattoo on her back
just below her waist
sports dragons and roses (Who doesn't have both?)
those roses possibly not edible.

A poster for "The Children's Guide to Astral Projection"
hangs on a wall. Why would the children want to go
somewhere else; they just got here?
Besides, it's challenge enough just being here,
really being at Mimosa, really seeing
the painted butterflies on the low pink table
or the tangerine orange of the walls
(not edible).

So let me feast with my eyes
on the delicate daises, pink and blue,
on the porcelain teacups from France!
And can you hear the avocados calling?
And why did I never notice that the base of the lamp
by the door – was an old horn?
There is music everywhere. Edible.

Maybe you thought a garden was only a garden,
not a menu, or that a café could not feed your dreams.
But nothing, no one's just one thing:
those shy accountants may be raging beasts in bed,
the angry lawyers soft as brie inside,

and those musicians may outside seem relaxed
but inside be as hard
as peanut brittle.

And though it's true you cannot eat the peonies
on the lamp shade at Mimosa,
or the paper baby chrysanthemums
that hang from the ceiling –
you can eat Tommy's gardens.

ANIMAL TALK

I'm at a table with Susan,
the Scottish healer whose Animal Rescuing
included four tiny horses yesterday, she says,
and with Daithi, an acupuncturist from Ireland
who used to tour with the Beatles.
We all live in Topanga now.

I mention the coyote I saw last Sunday
standing right in the middle of my road
as if he owned it, the dead dog limp in his jaws
(or was it my neighbor's big cat?)
and Daithi remembers the coyotes and
the mountain lion
that ate all his chickens (not one left).

Susan describes her own encounter with a coyote
that grabbed one of her dogs in his mouth and then
after what seemed his long decision-making process,
and despite the semi-circle of five coyotes behind him,
finally dropped her dog right in front of her;

and we sit here at Mimosa and talk,
my fluffy white dog safe at my side
far from the canyon predators.
Safe.

A SHIRT

I compliment Jack (a regular)
on his brown and green
cotton flannel shirt
and he answers
"Tryin' to stay cozy in this world."

We all want cozy.
Who doesn't?

Sometimes a flannel shirt will do it,
sometimes a happy meal with friends
in a toasty kitchen.

Sometimes it's a hug or being curled up
with your favorite curled up cat or dog.

And sometimes –
it's a café.

LIMERICKISH

I notice that Topangans here
All have more than one career.
I cannot say just why they do,
And frankly I don't have a clue,
It's just what these Topangans do.

There's the doctor and the dancer who
Both will write a song or two,
The activist who takes a stand
Who's also playing in a band,
The chef who's selling fancy shirts,
The healer who keeps building yurts.

This partial list I know is not
The longer list of who does what.
But people here, I think it's clear –
They all have more than one career
And some have three careers or four
Or five or six or even more.

No matter why it may be true,
It's just what these Topangans do.

LETTING GO THE METRONOME

Without warning, this morning at the café,
my dog jumps onto the bench across the narrow aisle
and rests his head on a stranger's purse, one leg
on her lap,
the other over her blue, white and black
striped cotton bag.
It looks like he's hugging her purse or her person;
a little encouragement and he's kissing her face.

It's Mimosa so she and I talk.
Young, pretty, she's a pianist and composer,
her husband, next to her, a pianist, composer
and conductor.
Catherine and Kim.
(What music, spontaneous, instantaneous, intuitive,
inspires my dog to make himself at home there?)

The three of us talk of Mozart,
of my play about Mozart's sister,
of my having studied at the Mozarteum in Salzburg
(I was going to be a concert pianist).
Now the couple's interested. I say my teacher there,
Heinz Scholz, was like a Nazi metronome,
his words like bullets, 'til all there was was:
"One. Two. Three. Four.
ONE! TWO! THREE! FOUR!"
the rhapsody and joy of the music
quite, quite gone.

"Metronomes should get us on course
and then be left behind," says Catherine,

while her husband insists he listens only to
his inner intuition when conducting,
and she remembers how, two years ago, her husband
touched her pregnant belly and he understood
how many heartbeats every minute played inside
(and now they have a healthy little girl they both adore!).

Me, I had my fill of metronomic orders growing up:
"Legs Together! One, Two! Get an A! Three. Four."
"Laugh, But Not Too Loud! One! Two!"
"KEEP THOSE SNEEZES QUIET, THREE, FOUR!!"

God bless Mimosa, so unlike the formal restaurants
I ate in, in New York, where still it's
NO DOGS ALLOWED and of course
Don't talk to the people at the next table!
"And never," insisted my mother, "blow your nose
in your napkin – at least if I am there,
or if anyone I know is there!"
(And don't kiss strangers –
as if we all didn't need a little extra love.)

How many coffees, shakes and muffins here
at this cafe
will it take for me to leave behind old metronomes,
to talk to strangers, wherever I am,
to stand up suddenly and dance in a café,
or anywhere, until I'm dancing only
to my own music....

JUGGLING

I practice my juggling here.
No one cares. I fit right in.
I've only had one lesson and want
another, the first was so much fun.
Oooh, la la! Those red, white and purple
bean bags in the air!
(the colors of the café's armchair
and the French aprons for sale against the wall!).

My juggled dog lands on the floor
from the turns in the palms of my hands.
Then UP goes his biscuit! DOWN goes his water!
UP fly his ears, DOWN his tongue!
And he rolls over on the floor
where the bean bags fell
(My juggling needs some work).

I notice that the art of juggling my life
is no less challenging: juggling my poems,
my coaching, my eating, my yoga,
my friendships, too, sometimes up in the air.
(Some friends even leave. More stay.)

I juggle the plumber, the handyman,
even a contractor complete with crew,
as I tend to a house where things get tired
and want to die
(never an easy place for anything or anyone).
I juggle the outside regulator, the indoor toilet,
leaks on window sills, with my deck falling

down the hillside
because of the shifting land (What isn't shifting?!).

Here at Café Mimosa I juggle my writing
with drinking my coffee with nodding at people
with talking to others and hugging still others
(but I can't when I'm writing, like now).
UP with my pen! DOWN with my coffee!
UP the Topanga Messenger!
DOWN The New York Times!
UP in the air the green embroidered pillow
from one couch to another to make sitting
really comfortable!

Who says I'm not a circus clown
(I actually was one)
or that Mimosa is not a circus –
Claire, its Ringmaster?
And wasn't that my little dog just now
prancing between my long and sturdy legs,
like the dog at the Big Apple Circus
running underneath the mighty Clydesdale
(always my favorite trick).
And who's that clown in the red cotton shirt
who barely saved himself from a perfect
PRATFALL, tripping over the dog leash
scarcely visible on the floor?

Who in here is not a clown?
Who is not a circus artist?
Who indeed is not a perfect
juggling clown!

DAVE LICHTEN, 1946–2015

Dave Lichten,
an odd man, furry, burry,
hair wild, spirit wild
played Spanish guitar
as well as the very, very,
very best of them.
Claire let him play here,
every afternoon those years ago,
always gave him lunch.

Every afternoon he played,
his body wrapped around his guitar
the way the café held us both,
Dave improvising, me dancing to his music
knowing it was safe to dance,
safe to make music, improvise freely,
kicking my legs high if I wanted
or pivoting on the ball of one foot, safe.

A true artist, he loved making art –
it could be a photograph, a guitar improvisation,
or a six-course, nuanced gourmet meal,
it didn't matter, he threw himself into it,

and, like a devoted holy man,
he was equally committed
to his mission for Topanga Fire Safety,
and even in the dead of night,
when the Santa Anas blew,
he drove the fire trails to keep us safe.
Safe.

DREAM CATCHERS

Unlike yesterday, suddenly, today,
on the orange wall opposite Claire's hats –
are dream catchers!

Strings of lace
or white feathers
hang off the mandala-like hoops,
some with shiny fabric flowers in the middle,
one has a sequined butterfly,
some have shells on their circumferences,
while others are pierced through with arrows,
a feather on one end,
a paper, polka-dotted, pointy cone at the other –

And I dream that all this could be
for our own flowering
our private dreaming
our own lacey sleep,
seemingly illusory voyages
that we can transform into new
hope.

HOW MANY LANGUAGES

How many languages are spoken here?
Spanish of course. French. Czech.
Portuguese, German. Italian, Hebrew.
We're a mini United Nations
but without discord or war zones,
without disaster areas,
without resolutions that can't be resolved,
without the future of world destruction
hanging in the balance.

OK, maybe there'll be a dispute over
the wrong kind of milk in a cappuccino
or at the worst an unwelcome flirt.
But never a pinch or a punch.

Woodrow Wilson would be proud.

A WEDDING

On a plane from New York
to return to Topanga,
I dream of the café – its warmth, gossip,
friendliness, dog friendliness,
of Claire of the long blonde hair,
and of the chocolate, chocolate-chip muffins
"sugar and gluten-free" – presumably.

I could get married there,
march down the aisle of the outdoor patio
with Dancer, my dog, my main squeeze,
my Laughter Hero, for a marriage: me to him, him to me,
maybe us to the café, Claire, and the customers.

I imagine Dancer and me walking solemnly
through the café's cathedral doorway
into the apse flooded with color and light,
and people nodding as we proceed
towards the altar of the counter,
Claire there, smiling priestess minister
ready to take our vows: to drink her coffee,
pay our bill, as my dog and I promise
to love, honor, cherish and obey each other
(the obeying mainly for Dancer).

No one objects, even though the air is always
rife with objection – to nuclear weapons,
government lies, community plans which
might involve a second traffic light (ABHORRENT!)

or Caltrans' proposal of pesticides (DESPICABLE!)
for roadside weeds, which we Topangans, if we must
will end up taking out ourselves.

And then the whole café pronounces us
"Squirrely Mutt" (Dancer part poodle, part bichon)
and "Chocolate Muffin Buying Dog Owner,"
presumably with license – not only for
my Special Support dog, but also for
Pleasure! Giggles!
Hugs! Applause!
SINGING, DANCING!

Dancer and I then take our honeymoon
in the red and gold striped armchair
where he sits with me, now on no one else's lap,
faithful, as we will be to each other
in sickness and in health until death us do part.

And who knows if he has dreamed of me
back at the Pet Resort awaiting my return,
because don't I always take him the best places –
the beach, and Bloomie's, and Jerry's Famous Deli!?

Perhaps he dreams of all the fun we've had
at Mimosa – of all the people petting him,
complementing his beauty, his handsomeness,
saying how cute he is, how well behaved,
of all the faces he has kissed there, and licked,
along with the crumbs off the floor,
or of the joy of rolling upside down on his head

on the grey cushioned couch, then onto his back
his legs stretched out, mouth opened wide laughing
wriggling and squiggling with joy.

But the wedding awaits us in Topanga
and first the airplane has to land and I need to set foot
on California soil, solid ground, ending this reverie,
this ceremonial riff among the clouds.

Back in New York, my sister had survived her surgery,
with flying colors, victorious – our getting together
almost like another wedding:
after years of a cold war, finally allowing ourselves
to love each other.
Marriages are everywhere, I guess.

CLOSING TIME

Five pm the café closes, and,
as at my yoga studio,
whoever is in charge sweeps up –
sometimes Al, sometimes Susan –
the end of the day like the end of a life
no debris left, the body and bones gone.

And what remains is the joy,
its ripples spinning into the world,
endlessly entering, a surge, a swell into the world
which remembers the joy,
reverberations of old laughter,
never forgotten conversations,
the thrill of meeting an old friend
or discovering a new one,
hearing an old joke
or eating a new and perfect soup.

And yes there has also been pain in the room --
after someone's heart has just been broken
or one of the regulars dies.
How many people have cried there on my shoulder,
tears which only bless our faces,
wash us clean like the café floor,
the clean table tops and kitchen surfaces,
water just a little like the Perriers
and Arrowheads for sale in the fridge,
special baptisms, all holy water,
like the special teas and coffees
or even the smoothies made to order.

But what remains is the joy, not the pain;
and maybe just a sip of Claire's new coffee
will make it right again.

PRESIDENTIAL ELECTION

i.

Election Day, November 8, 2016

10 AM
Mimosa throbs, as if indeed charged
with the pulse of the canyon
if not the whole city or country.

On the outside it may look like business as usual:
I ask for a handyman to caulk my tub,
wonder who would know how to re-hinge a cabinet door,
someone else needs his house painted,
these small comforts important today,
a day terrifying for many.

Julie McNally and I try to make a date to go dancing
(the free-form kind where you improvise, don't need a partner,
and can end up on the floor
seeming to writhe around with a perfect stranger).
Gail McTune, Master Nutritionist, eats her two
hard-boiled eggs with olive oil and salt.
(Really?!?!)

I've bought the prefab salad with sliced chicken and cheese,
pour its raspberry dressing on the lettuce and tomatoes
and share the chicken with Dancer,
though he gets all the cheese
(my diet dairy-free).
I crunch the carrot slivers hoping for better vision

to see, more clearly, where the country really is.

Claire's blond hair hangs loose halfway down her back today,
the tresses wavy, as I imagine Goldilocks' were,
The Three Bears everywhere -
and though one chair here may be a bit too hard
and the red and orange pillow too soft,
still, my cappuccino with hemp milk is
"Just right."

On the surface it may seem like any other day
but the air feels tight, most people scared, sad.
Still, there's Timmy typing a script on his Mac,
and Adam possibly polishing a workshop proposal,
maybe the one to teach men how to be men.
I don't ask. Not today.

My dog too feels the anxiety, seems to need
to hump every single dog that enters,
so there's an unusual amount of unwieldy barking.
He even jumps a foot in the air
to reach the chihuahua under one of Gail's arms,
as if contact for him too
were singularly necessary today, even as countries
all over the world metaphorically hold their breath,
(never healthy for anything or anybody)
anxious about the election.

I'm determined to get to Yoga,
to take its extended deep breaths,
as if this were my vote for the survival of us all,

afraid of a candidate who mentions nuclear weapons
as if they were toys he might enjoy –
on an impulse.

Part of me is weeping for America,
everyone so anxious. I wonder if there'll be more
car accidents today than usual, more road rage from fear,
less paying attention, everyone only focused on the vote.

I come to this café for comfort, company, community
and marvel that things and people here
touch me so deeply that I have to write about them;
perhaps it's no accident that Tommy wrote his Mimosa song here,
and James Chressanthis has begun to shoot a film about it.
WE ELECT TO BE HERE.
Of course. Here we feel safe, away from
ballot boxes probably not rigged.

Earlier this morning, in the Topanga sunshine,
I voted for a new president, a woman;
and now I come here nervous of the outcome
knowing how so many people in our country are angry,
unhappy, murderously angry, murderously unhappy,
even hopeless and desolate.

There's a red, white and blue sticker reading
"I VOTED"
glued in front of my heart,
the sticker shaped like an ellipse –
as one imagines our planet circling the sun,
even as our election, like the sun or moon,

pulls its own myriad of tides –
the tsunami of climate change no more a myth
than that the earth revolves around the sun
or that the world isn't flat.

I leave Mimosa after an hour for Yoga
as if in class I could find some peaceful inner lake
while the whole world and my entire nervous system
are up in arms. I'm scared
if Trump's elected he'll make the poor poorer,
disenfranchise anyone not Christian and white.

I tell this to Adam, he tells me not to worry, hadn't I computed
the math of the Electoral College proving Hillary will win?
No, I hadn't. Silly me.
Still, I cannot help but think
we do not live by math alone.

ii.
Two days later.

Trump elected.
Some of us, prescient, often too sensitive,
were right to doubt the math.
Poets, artists, me, we fear his prejudice
against minorities, a minority ourselves ....

Not everyone who goes to Mimosa is a Democrat
but this afternoon the few stragglers here are,
and scared and sad. Some people think the world will end.
School children are crying in their classrooms,

college kids cut classes, protest in the streets.
I remember when I was growing up, children barely cared.

How to surrender to what IS –
even to the uneven pillows on the couch
or the dense sweetness of a muffin?

Me, I elect to be kind,
to surround myself with people who are likewise kind.
I can only hope Trump will show the qualities
I choose to elect for myself.
I elect to be generous,
even to give without expecting anything in return.
I elect to champion men
who do not grab unwilling women.
I vote for compassion to Trump followers,
to understand their desperation for a better life,
even understand the impulse to be prejudiced
against those unlike myself.

Still, I know we are all part of the human race,
our DNA the same as the ancient stars
and in that way we're all the same, indivisible,
one country, under God, with liberty and justice for all.
And who in fact is not a minority unto himself?
And how, despite everyone's inevitable fear of
The Different,
how do we battle more love into the world!?

Being in the café, and not alone,
somehow feeds us all with invisible courage,
provides ineffable safety, security, sanctuary,

all maybe stepping stones to new strength
not to take this lying down.

I look out Mimosa's wall-sized window,
and across the boulevard I see the huge and sturdy mountains,
there for centuries,
bare rock and brush, chaparral, sumac, coastal oaks,
through the faintly painted tree on the window.
I choose to focus on the trees,
even the young eucalyptus on the patio by the front door.
I see and sense how their branches reach up
maybe to God, maybe to heaven, maybe just up,
think how we breathe in their oxygen
and choose life.

MY THANKS

My thanks to Jimmy Roberts, the wonderful poet and composer, to whom I happened to send the first poem in this book. He gave me such a sweet review, that the poem and the review must have stayed buried, but not forgotten, in my brain until Tommy Teeple, six months later, happened to sing me his Mimosa song and this book was born. So thank you, Tommy. And Jimmy, for all your inspiration, support and friendship.

My heartfelt and eternal thanks to The Magnificent Four who always carefully read my work before I am brave enough to put it into the world: Rachel Chodorov, Dolly Gordon, Pam Shaw and Jennifer Strom. Endless and sincere thanks also to my amazing helpers: the supremely talented and multi-talented Alex Dennett; the smart and ebullient Joan Alperin; and the steady and dear Karen Roberts. They not only typed my endless and exacting revisions, but also offered and continue to offer support and wisdom beyond the call of duty.

My thanks to Joanna Gunst Grzymkowski for her balanced vision and grounded smarts; to Ellen Gales, Joyce Wisdom and Bob Gordon for their good eyes and generous spirits; to Emily Edelman who is, and has always been, ready to help; and to my special yoga teachers, Sibyl Buck and Annmarie Soul, in whose classes I got ideas for this book and who even provided a safe, if unusual space where I could write them down.

Thanks, finally, to Terry Belanger, who has been there, unflaggingly, as a friend and collaborator, with his own special genius, stubbornness, taste, integrity, generosity and passion, for more than half a century.

ABOUT THE AUTHOR

A finalist for a CAPS Grant in Poetry from the National Endowment of the Arts, Jane is the author of *Dogs in Topanga* and *Poems of The Laughing Buddha*, four of which you can see and hear her read on YouTube, where you can also hear her read two poems from *Café Mimosa in Topanga*.

Commissioned by the Kennedy Center in Washington D.C. to write and perform the one-woman play, *Reminiscences of Mozart by His Sister*, Jane also performed it at Lincoln Center in New York. Her one-woman play in verse, *Miriam's Dance*, about Moses' sister, was produced in New York and Los Angeles. Her most recent play, *A Radical Friendship*, a two-hander about Martin Luther King Jr. and Rabbi Abraham Heschel, has been seen in New York and Los Angeles starring Ed Asner.

Jane's best-selling self-help book, *Acting Techniques for Everyday Life: Look and Feel Self-Confident in Difficult Real-Life Situations*, and its accompanying deck of cards, *Perform At Your Best: Acting Techniques for Business, Social, and Personal Success*, won the Gold Axiom Business Book Award. She teaches workshops based on the book at universities and corporations, to veterans for their job interviews (through the MVAT Foundation, www.mvat.org) and teaches privately.

Jane's first one-woman play, *Dear Nobody*, co-authored with Terry Belanger, was nominated for an Obie, ran for a year Off-Broadway, was produced on CBS, and toured to London and all over the United States. Also in New York she starred in her three-character play *Jane Avril*. Her one acts include: *Bats in the Belfry*, produced at the Spoleto Festival; *Cornucopia*, winner of

The University of St. Thomas One Act Play Competition; and *Norman and the Killer*, a co-adaptation for PBS.

Jane has acted in movies (*Rocky I, Rocky II, Rocky V, Arachnophobia*); on TV (*ER, The Heidi Chronicles*); on Broadway (*Richard III, Morning, Noon and Night*); and played The Clown Ringmaster with Circus Flora.

For more information go to www.janemarlarobbins.com

A RECORDING

You can hear Jane Marla Robbins read two of the poems from this book and hear Tommy Teeple sing his song, *Conversation: Mimosa*, on YouTube. (Go to: www.youtube.com/Café Mimosa in Topanga).

Nick Garside recorded the poems and the song, and added guitar and piano to the song. He was the recording engineer for the bands James, Hothouse Flowers and The Durutti Column.

Tommy Teeple wrote the music and lyrics for the song, and accompanies himself on the guitar. His band, Tommy Teeple and The Quantum Hitch-Hikers, has made five albums, all of which you can find on his website TommyTeeple.com. The band has often performed at Café Mimosa. Of course.

Made in the USA
Lexington, KY
12 June 2017